Also by Donald Revell

Collections of Poetry

Tantivy, Alice James Books, 2012
The Bitter Withy, Alice James Books, 2009
A Thief of Strings, Alice James Books, 2007
Pennyweight Windows: New & Selected Poems,
Alice James Books, 2005
My Mojave, Alice James Books, 2003
Arcady, Wesleyan University Press, 2002
There Are Three, Wesleyan University Press, 1998
Beautiful Shirt, Wesleyan University Press, 1994
Erasures, Wesleyan University Press, 1992
New Dark Ages, Wesleyan University Press, 1990
The Gaza of Winter, University of Georgia Press, 1988
From the Abandoned Cities, Harper & Row, 1983

Prose

The Art of Attention: A Poet's Eye, Graywolf Press, 2007
Invisible Green: Selected Prose, Omnidawn Publishing, 2005

Translations

Last Verses, by Jules Laforgue, Omnidawn Publishing, 2011
The Illuminations, by Arthur Rimbaud, Omnidawn Publishing, 2009
A Season in Hell, by Arthur Rimbaud, Omnidawn Publishing, 2007
*The Self-Dismembered Man: Selected Later Poems of
Guillaume Apollinaire*, Wesleyan University Press, 2004
Alcools: Poems of Guillaume Apollinaire, Wesleyan University Press, 1995

Songs without Words

Songs without Words

by

Paul Verlaine

Translated by
Donald Revell

OMNIDAWN PUBLISHING
RICHMOND, CALIFORNIA
2013

Cover Art: *The Death of Pierrot* (1896)
by Aubrey Beardsley (1872–1898)
From *The Savoy* (magazine), Volume 4, August 1898

Book cover and interior design by Ken Keegan

Offset printed in the United States
by Edwards Brothers Malloy, Ann Arbor, Michigan
on Glatfelter Natures Natural 55# Recycled 30% PCW
Acid Free Archival Quality FSC Certified Paper
with Rainbow FSC Certified Colored End Papers

Cataloguing-in-Publication Data is available from the Library of Congress

Original French Edition

Romances sans paroles:
Ariettes oubliées, Paysages belges, Birds in the Night, Aquarelles,
by Paul Verlaine (Paris: Léon Vanier, 1891).

Translation published by
Omnidawn Publishing, Richmond, California
www.omnidawn.com   (510) 237-5472

10 9 8 7 6 5 4 3 2 1

ISBN: 978-1-890650-87-2

Acknowledgments

The translations of "Je devine…" and "Dans l'interminable" first appeared in *A Public Space*, Issue 16 (2012).

The "Translator's Afterword" first appeared as "Verlaine Afterwards" in the *Tributes* section of the Poetry Society of America's web site.

for

Jeffrey Peters & Dona Shatford Peters

Table of Contents

A Prior Enchantment

At the cemetery, she leant over the grave: "Verlaine! All your friends are here!" A magnificent cry. And that was why he loved her.

—*Verlaine: A Biography*

So observed Maurice Barrès, one of Verlaine's several eulogists, in a notebook entry for January 10, 1896—the day of Verlaine's funeral, a day of light snow falling out of clear blue skies onto Paris and onto the hundreds of mourners who followed the coffin from a dirty courtyard in the rue Descartes to High Mass at Saint-Étienne-du-Mont (Gabriel Fauré was the organist), and from there to the graveside. "She" was Eugénie Krantz, the very last of Verlaine's many vivid, unparalleled enchantments. In the days of the Second Empire, whose throes and collapse brought Arthur Rimbaud to Verlaine's door, she had been a great beauty, a music-hall starlet called *Ninie Mouton*. Verlaine met her in the year of Rimbaud's death, 1891, in a wine shop. By then, Eugénie was a prostitute and Verlaine already dying of more illnesses than his devoted, unpaid physicians could number. It was in Eugénie's little rooms that he would make his last confession, receive the last sacraments, and die.

Enchantment was the motive force of Paul Verlaine, man and poet. His worst moments and most perfect hours were equally sacramental. In life, enchantment made for a series of fanatic devotions, erotic and spiritual, absolute in their addictedness and absolute also in their disaster. In poetry, it made for exquisite candor, a music whose purity, whether sounded on a lyre or barrel organ, remains matchless—almost hermetic, entirely its own. In *A Certain World*, W. H. Auden offers a capsule history of enchantment which might well serve as a critical biography of Verlaine, more accurate both before and after the fact than any translation.

All true enchantments fade in time. Sooner or later we must walk alone in faith. When this happens, we are tempted, either to deny our vision, to say that it must have been an illusion and, in consequence, grow hard-hearted

13

and cynical, or to make futile attempts to recover our
vision by force, i.e. by alcohol or drugs.

Save for a few fantastic intervals, Verlaine walked alone, his faith
indistinguishable from catastrophe. And yet, somehow, catastrophe only
softened his heart. Both the angels and the demons of his nature were
eternal ingenues. In life, his futility was as absolute as the Vision that
drove it. He was the perfect alcoholic, addicted to the story of himself
and to the substances—absinthe, God, and poetry—that made his story
true. In the poems themselves, however, futility is simply unimaginable.
Certainly, some of the books are better than others; some passages
are crystalline, while others are paste and bathetic. Yet not even the
most embarrassing passages betray an instant of doubt. In the poetry,
perfection outspeeds disgrace, sometimes by force of enchantment,
sometimes by faith alone. Verlaine was the living embodiment of
Rimbaud's famous dictum: *Il faut être absolument moderne*. Disgrace is
refractory; enchantment is for Now, and Now, and Now.

Among the fantastic intervals, nevertheless and because, Paul
Verlaine once surely walked alone with *the* alone, i.e. with Rimbaud.
This was his double enchantment, an arcadia of poems laid upon an
arcadia of flesh, a fabulous *dédoublement*. For twenty-two months
(September 1871–July 1873), Verlaine's life and art traveled together
in a single, irreproachable catastrophe. For twenty-two months, his
Vision had a name, and was no one. The days and the poetry of the
days confided to one another an intimacy futility could not find, in
measures without precedent or plan. In English, we might reference
such as "ditties of no tone"; in French, they are *Romances sans paroles*,
songs without words.

There is a notorious, inexplicit narrative which serves as armature
and incentive to Verlaine's most famous collection; this narrative
begins at one threshold with a most remarkable appearance, and ends
at another, in whose deep shadow disappearance multiplies into the
stuff of legend. The first threshold is a Parisian doorstep, entryway
to Verlaine's happy marriage to Mathilde, his child-bride. The other
is a prison gate in Belgium. Upon the first, Rimbaud appears out
of the Ardennes with his enormous hands, cold blue eyes, and "Le
Bateau ivre." At the other, a gunshot Rimbaud disappears into travel,

renunciation and commerce; Mathilde, along with Verlaine's honor and only son, disappears into monumental rancor; and prisoner Verlaine, convicted gunman and sodomite, undergoes a jailhouse conversion, careful all the while to orchestrate the piecemeal music of twenty-two months into *Romances sans paroles*.

Between thresholds, the poems account for themselves and for their author, proving, as always, that life is elsewhere. In pastiche whose precisions outmode Modernism in advance, *Songs without Words* juxtaposes sodden byways in Normandy with noisy corners of Soho, Belgian shepherds with Paddington undines. Shipboard stumbles beside roughshod. Ecstasy joins hands with abasement to walk on clouds. The sovereign timeline is Verlaine's revolutionized line, attenuated and then sprawled. The poetry of Rimbaud is revolutionary by nature, Verlaine's revolutionary by design. In *Songs without Words*, catastrophized together, nature and design intertwine. They fuck each other clean, and their postcoital embrace is innocence, which Rimbaud called "Christmas on earth!" and Verlaine calls simply "*le frais oubli*," the new oblivion. A sentence from C. Day Lewis comes to mind just now: "new, dominantly sensual love creates the illusion of innocence." And then immediately another, much earlier English poet intervenes: "It was no dream. I lay broad waking." Thomas Wyatt is nearer to Verlaine than Lewis. The phrase "le frais oubli" appears quite early in *Songs without Words*, in a poem beginning "Il faut, voyez-vous, nous pardonner les choses." New innocence commands pardon, up front and ever after. In Arcady, the very thingness of things, "les choses," insists that it be so. Design becomes nature in Verlaine's declarative, and so on through the prison gate at Mons.

> "If poetry is not absolution"—he whispered to himself—"then we can expect pity from nowhere else."
> —Yannis Ritsos

Instantly, or so it seems, literature forgave Arthur Rimbaud for being no one but himself. High time, then, that Paul Verlaine be forgiven for being Verlaine, the poet of *Romances sans paroles* and not of *Une Saison en Enfer*. Honestly, I would love to propose that Rimbaud and Verlaine together constitute a single poet, perhaps even *the* poet. But as Meister Eckhart would say of matters better broached

15

in Heaven, of things like rivers running straight uphill and pine forests marching into cathedrals, "I will not speak of that for now." Better now to read them, both of them, and also together as they traveled in *Songs without Words*. Reading is absolution. Anyone who reads is a jailhouse convert.

———

God loves all men but is enchanted by none.
—W. H. Auden, *A Certain World*

As the undertakers were about to bear away the coffin, Eugénie said: "Someone's taken his religious book. If they don't give it back at once, I'll create a commotion at the grave."
—*Verlaine: A Biography*

No commotion was necessary. The anonymous souvenir hunters returned Verlaine's missal to his hands, and ceremonies went forward. At the graveside, life and enchantment go their separate ways: the one to God, the other to posterity, which we must and always mistake for the present day. In the poem beginning "*Il faut, voyez-vous, nous pardonner les choses*," Verlaine concludes with this extended imperative:

Let's be children, let's be little girls,
Ignorant as air and astonished by everything,
Transparent as the air on apple boughs,
Ignorant even of forgiveness shining down.

Enchantments fade over time. But forgiveness, being *absolument moderne*, absolutely modern, carries Eden a baby step further, and then another step further still. The roughshod travelers of *Romances sans paroles* show the havoc and the way.

Works Cited

W. H. Auden. *A Certain World*. New York: The Viking Press, 1970.

C. Day Lewis. *The Buried Day*. New York: Harper & Brothers, 1960.

Joanna Richardson. *Verlaine: A Biography*. New York: The Viking
    Press, 1971.

Yannis Ritsos (trans. Paul Merchant)."The Poet's Place" from *Another
    Republic* (eds. Charles Simic & Mark Strand), New York: Ecco, 1984.

Romances sans paroles

by

Paul Verlaine

Songs without Words

Translated by

Donald Revell

Ariettes oubliées

Forgotten Showtunes

I

Le vent dans la plaine
Suspend son haleine.
—Favart

C'est l'extase langoureuse,
C'est la fatigue amoureuse,
C'est tous les frissons des bois
Parmi l'étreinte des brises,
C'est, vers les ramures grises,
Le chœur des petites voix.

Ô le frêle et frais murmure!
Cela gazouille et susurre,
Cela ressemble au cri doux
Que l'herbe agitée expire…
Tu dirais, sous l'eau qui vire,
Le roulis sourd des cailloux.

Cette âme qui se lamente
En cette plainte dormante,
C'est la nôtre, n'est-ce pas?
La mienne, dis, et la tienne,
Dont s'exhale l'humble antienne
Par ce tiède soir, tout bas?

I

The wind on the plain
Is breathless.

—Favart

Old ecstasy, this
Amorous fatigue, these
Woods trembling
In the broken grip of the wind,
While in the white treetops
Tiny voices sing.

Frail susurrus, a cooling
Gasp and murmur,
Ghost of an outcry,
Call it the bad sleep of the grass
Or a sound of creek water
Troubled by stones.

The sound is us—
My soul inside of yours,
Submissive, antiphonal, twinned,
A lament beneath
An anguish, a hot night,
Not a breath of air.

II

Je devine, à travers un murmure,
Le contour subtil des voix anciennes
Et dans les lueurs musiciennes,
Amour pâle, une aurore future!

Et mon âme et mon cœur en délires
Ne sont plus qu'une espèce d'œil double
Où tremblote à travers un jour trouble
L'ariette, hélas! de toutes lyres!

Ô mourir de cette mort seulette
Que s'en vont, cher amour qui t'épeures,
Balançant jeunes et vieilles heures!
Ô mourir de cette escarpolette!

II

I can barely discern,
Through a murmur,
Erotic polyphony—
A diaphane, a daybreak.

My heart is of two minds,
My soul is a murk and mis-
Apprehension of arias,
The world's small voices.

Frightening to die alone
Death coming in pretty ribbons
Flickering now for all time
In the voices of children on swings.

III

Il pleure dans mon cœur
Comme il pleut sur la ville,
Quelle est cette langueur
Qui pénètre mon cœur?

Ô bruit doux de la pluie
Par terre et sur les toits!
Pour un cœur qui s'ennuie
Ô le chant de la pluie!

Il pleure sans raison
Dans ce cœur qui s'écœure.
Quoi! nulle trahison?
Ce deuil est sans raison.

C'est bien la pire peine
De ne savoir pourquoi,
Sans amour et sans haine,
Mon cœur a tant de peine!

III

Soft rain falls on the town.
—Arthur Rimbaud

Warm tears in my heart
Today, like the rain
On the town. It goes
On somehow.

Soft sound of rain
On rooftops, on the ground!
In a cold heart,
The song of rain!

Useless tears,
Heartsick still.
Fantastic betrayals
Today like rain.

The worst of it,
Not loving, not hating,
Not understanding it,
Such pain!

IV

Il faut, voyez-vous, nous pardonner les choses.
De cette façon nous serons bien heureuses,
Et si notre vie a des instants moroses,
Du moins nous serons, n'est-ce pas? deux pleureuses.

Ô que nous mêlions, âmes sœurs que nous sommes,
À nos vœux confus la douceur puérile
De cheminer loin des femmes et des hommes,
Dans le frais oubli de ce qui nous exile.

Soyons deux enfants, soyons deux jeunes filles
Éprises de rien et de tout étonnées,
Qui s'en vont pâlir sous les chastes charmilles,
Sans même savoir qu'elles sont pardonnées.

IV

Don't you see, and you must see it, we must
Be forgiven: from the sunshine of forgiveness
Comes our joy; out of the murk of the bad days,
Well, on bad days we bitch and moan.

Infant souls, voluptuary sisters
Gone far away into soft confusion,
Unknown to men, unknown to women,
We are a new oblivion.

Let's be children, let's be little girls,
Ignorant as air and astonished by everything,
Transparent as the air on apple boughs,
Ignorant even of forgiveness shining down.

V

Son joyeux, importun d'un clavecin sonore.
—Pétrus Borel

Le piano que baise une main frêle
Luit dans le soir rose et gris vaguement,
Tandis qu'avec un très léger bruit d'aile
Un air bien vieux, bien faible et bien charmant
Rôde discret, épeuré quasiment,
Par le boudoir longtemps parfumé d'Elle.

Qu'est-ce que c'est que ce berceau soudain
Qui lentement dorlote mon pauvre être?
Que voudrais-tu de moi, doux chant badin?
Qu'as-tu voulu, fin refrain incertain
Qui vas tantôt mourir vers la fenêtre
Ouverte un peu sur le petit jardin?

V

Importunate, happy sound of a harpsichord.
—Pétrus Borel

Piano keys stroked by reedy hands
Glow in the half-light, pink into gray,
While all the while the faintest sound
Of wings, an old song, almost brittle,
Drifts towards silence—the absolute
Perfume, the eternal, unwelcome She.

Account, if you can, for this sudden cradle.
Explain this febrile lullaby to my bones.
What game are we playing? Who's touching me?
I don't understand. I only see
Fine hairs of music lifted by a breeze
Coming into the room out of the garden.

VI

C'est le chien de Jean de Nivelle
Qui mord sous l'œil même du guet
Le chat de la mère Michel;
François-les-bas-bleus s'en égaie.

La lune à l'écrivain public
Dispense sa lumière obscure
Où Médor avec Angélique
Verdissent sur le pauvre mur.

Et voici venir La Ramée
Sacrant en bon soldat du Roi.
Sous son habit blanc mal famé,
Son cœur ne se tient pas de joie!

Car la boulangère… —Elle? —Oui dame!
Bernant Lustucru, son vieil homme,
A tantôt couronné sa flamme…
Enfants, *Dominus vobiscum!*

Place! en sa longue robe bleue
Toute en satin qui fait frou-frou,
C'est une impure, palsembleu!
Dans sa chaise qu'il faut qu'on loue,

Fût-on philosophe ou grigou,
Car tant d'or s'y relève en bosse
Que ce luxe insolent bafoue
Tout le papier de monsieur Loss!

Arrière, robin crotté! place,
Petit courtaud, petit abbé,
Petit poète jamais las
De la rime non attrapée!

VI

Johnny Nivell's shameless mutt
Is mauling Mother Mischa's cat.
The worthless watchman watches while
Frankie Blue-Shoes laughs at that.

An illiterate moon is nearly full
Behind the dozing notary.
Fido pees on the poorhouse wall.
Poor, dying puss-cat's turning green.

And who comes here, like a walking tree,
In the apron of a butcher's boy?
It's foul-mouthed Ramey, proud as can be,
In his gore and postcoital joy.

Joy in the baker's wife—none other!
Even Ben the Retard's done her,
Stoked her fire, stuffed her oven.
On your knees, my children! Pray for her.

Look out, now. A courtesan, forsooth,
Passes in syphilitic state,
In virgin blue and satin frou-frou,
In a carriage any man, saint

Or skinflint, would gladly die for. Such
Extravagance, when boldly flaunted,
Bankrupts God himself. So much
For virtue, children! Sin's what's wanted.

Step aside there, dumpy dickhead,
Little good-for-nothing friar,
Half-baked bumptious versifier.
Haven't you heard? Poetry is dead.

Voici que la nuit vraie arrive…
Cependant jamais fatigué
D'être inattentif et naïf
François-les-bas-bleus s'en égaie.

This is the dark night of the soul.
This is the dog that killed the cat.
This is the story Rimbaud told,
And Frankie Blue-Shoes laughs at that.

VII

Ô triste, triste était mon âme
À cause, à cause d'une femme.

Je ne me suis pas consolé
Bien que mon cœur s'en soit allé,

Bien que mon cœur, bien que mon âme
Eussent fui loin de cette femme.

Je ne me suis pas consolé,
Bien que mon cœur s'en soit allé.

Et mon cœur, mon cœur trop sensible
Dit à mon âme: Est-il possible,

Est-il possible, —le fût-il, —
Ce fier exil, ce triste exil?

Mon âme dit à mon cœur: Sais-je
Moi-même, que nous veut ce piège

D'être présents bien qu'exilés,
Encore que loin en allés?

VII

Was oh my soul was sad because
Of a woman was sad because

Washed far away and gone my heart
Unhelped I stay although far gone

My heart a stranger and my soul too
Far gone to other worlds although

Unhelped I inconsolable
Stay here although my heart is gone.

My heart goes on to speak
Saying pain and impossible

To live oh my soul and soul speaks
Saying proud exile sorrowful

Exile nothing else. Where are we?
A mug's game a snare and from here

Again and once again as far
Together as strange we stay here.

VIII

Dans l'interminable
Ennui de la plaine
La neige incertaine
Luit comme du sable.

Le ciel est de cuivre
Sans lueur aucune
On croirait voir vivre
Et mourir la lune.

Comme des nuées
Flottent gris les chênes
Des forêts prochaines
Parmi les buées.

Le ciel est de cuivre
Sans lueur aucune
On croirait voir vivre
Et mourir la lune.

Corneille poussive
Et vous, les loups maigres,
Par ces bises aigres
Quoi donc vous arrive?

Dans l'interminable
Ennui de la plaine
La neige incertaine
Luit comme du sable.

VIII

Interminably,
Like sand, uncertain snow
Flattens the plain and gleams
Mirror-glass underground.

Not gleaming at all,
The sky is a scrap heap
Where the moon lives,
Where the moon dies.

Some trees, they might
Be oak trees, each
In a cloud of its own,
Float towards France.

Not gleaming at all,
The sky is a scrap heap
Where the moon lives,
Where the moon dies.

Wheezing blackbird, wolf-pack
All skin and bones in the bitter
Gales of midwinter,
What's to become of you?

Interminably,
Like sand, uncertain snow
Flattens the plain and gleams
Mirror-glass underground.

IX

L'ombre des arbres dans la rivière embrumée
    Meurt comme de la fumée,
Tandis qu'en l'air, parmi les ramures réelles,
    Se plaignent les tourterelles.

Combien, ô voyageur, ce paysage blême
    Te mira blême toi-même,
Et que tristes pleuraient dans les hautes feuillées
    Tes espérances noyées!

Mai, Juin 1872

IX

The nightingale who, from a high branch, looks down into
his image in the river, feels himself falling. He is at the very
top of an oak tree, and still he is afraid of drowning.
—Cyrano de Bergerac

Shadows of trees on the misted river
    Evanesce.
Overhead, in green, actual branches,
    Ringdoves grieve.

Oh traveler, this fading picturesque
    Mirrors death.
And overhead, in the drowning branches,
    All hope dies.

May, June 1872

Paysages belges

Belgian Landscapes

Walcourt

Briques et tuiles,
Ô les charmants
Petits asiles
Pour les amants!

Houblons et vignes,
Feuilles et fleurs,
Tentes insignes
Des francs buveurs!

Guinguettes claires,
Bières, clameurs,
Servantes chères
À tous fumeurs!

Gares prochaines,
Gais chemins grands…
Quelles aubaines,
Bons juifs errants!

Juillet 1873

Walcourt

Brickwork, tiles,
All the charms,
Makeshift lovers
Safe and warm.

Hops and vines,
Leaves and flowers,
Shantytown
Drunk at all hours.

Roadside taverns,
Barrels, blather,
Shapes in the smoke
And friendly laughter.

The depot's next door,
The streets never sleep…
Dear Wandering Jews,
Good luck and Godspeed.

July 1873

Charleroi

Dans l'herbe noire
Les Kobolds vont.
Le vent profond
Pleure, on veut croire.

Quoi donc se sent?
L'avoine siffle.
Un buisson gifle
L'œil au passant.

Plutôt des bouges
Que des maisons.
Quels horizons
De forges rouges!

On sent donc quoi?
Des gares tonnent,
Les yeux s'étonnent,
Où Charleroi?

Parfums sinistres!
Qu'est-ce que c'est?
Quoi bruissait
Comme des sistres?

Sites brutaux!
Oh! votre haleine,
Sueur humaine,
Cris des métaux!

Dans l'herbe noire
Les Kobolds vont.
Le vent profond
Pleure, on veut croire.

Charleroi

In the black grass,
Goblins dream.
You might almost believe
The air was screaming.

What was that?
It burned my eye.
Black straw and cinders
Fallen from the sky.

No houses, only
Shacks and smoke
And, behind the smoke,
A furnace glow.

Where's Charleroi?
I can hear machinery,
But I see no town.
Where's Charleroi?

A smell of sulfur.
Voices raised in anger
But without words.
A smell of sulfur.

Desolation.
Tailings sweat
And break like glass
Under my feet.

In the black grass,
Goblins dream.
I believe it.
The air is screaming.

Bruxelles
simples fresques

I

La fuite est verdâtre et rose
Des collines et des rampes,
Dans un demi-jour de lampes
Qui vient brouiller toute chose.

L'or sur les humbles abîmes,
Tout doucement s'ensanglante,
Des petits arbres sans cimes,
Où quelque oiseau faible chante.

Triste à peine tant s'effacent
Ces apparences d'automne.
Toutes mes langueurs rêvassent,
Que berce l'air monotone.

Brussels
simple frescos

I

The road out of town is rose-hued,
Changing over to green in the foothills.
Under the soft confusion of lamplight,
Day becomes night.

Very slowly, gold changes to blood-red
In the roadside shrines.
Out of the disappearing trees,
One bird sings a little while longer.

I am sad, yes, but only a little,
And now my sadness itself begins
To dream into the deep phantoms of autumn,
Cradled by the stillness of the air.

II

L'allée est sans fin
Sous le ciel, divin
D'être pâle ainsi!
Sais-tu qu'on serait
Bien sous le secret
De ces arbres-ci?

Des messieurs bien mis,
Sans nul doute amis
Des Royers-Collards,
Vont vers le château.
J'estimerais beau
D'être ces vieillards.

Le château, tout blanc
Avec, à son flanc,
Le soleil couché,
Les champs à l'entour…
Oh! que notre amour
N'est-il là niché!

Estaminet du Jeune Renard, août 1872

II

The path is endless
Under heaven,
Holy, pale as linen.
Say it! We'd be happy
Here, underneath
The secret of these trees.

Elegant men, surely
Friends of the gentry,
Climb the white steps
Into the chateau.
I'd like to be old
And walking beside them.

At the moment of sunset,
The chateau and broad lawns
Turn blindingly white.
The near distances shimmer.
If only our love
Could kennel here!

The Jeune Renard estaminet, August 1872

Bruxelles
chevaux de bois

Par Saint-Gille,
Viens nous-en,
Mon agile
Alezan.
                —Victor Hugo

Tournez, tournez, bons chevaux de bois,
Tournez cent tours, tournez mille tours,
Tournez souvent et tournez toujours,
Tournez, tournez au son des hautbois.

Le gros soldat, la plus grosse bonne
Sont sur vos dos comme dans leur chambre;
Car, en ce jour, au bois de la Cambre,
Les maîtres sont tous deux en personne.

Tournez, tournez, chevaux de leur cœur,
Tandis qu'autour de tous vos tournois
Clignote l'œil du filou sournois,
Tournez au son du piston vainqueur.

C'est ravissant comme ça vous soûle
D'aller ainsi dans ce cirque bête!
Bien dans le ventre et mal dans la tête,
Du mal en masse et du bien en foule.

Tournez, tournez, sans qu'il soit besoin
D'user jamais de nuls éperons
Pour commander à vos galops ronds,
Tournez, tournez, sans espoir de foin

Brussels
wooden horses

Tally-ho
To St. Giles,
My beauty,
We go.
          —Victor Hugo

Around and go round, you gaudy
Horses one hundred times, a thousand
Times go around again and for always
Go round for as long as the music plays.

The enormous cadet, the jiggling housemaid
Can ride you all day and kiss if they like,
For the captain has gone and taken the mistress
To fashionable woods with a blanket and wine.

Round and go round, you horses of heartstrings,
While all the while at the edge of your whirling,
In the raucous distraction Calliope makes,
Pickpockets ply their eagle-eyed trade.

Wonderful merely to wobble like drunkards
In carnival noise and animal glee:
Bad for the brain but good for the belly.
A mob is a mess, but a crowd is a spree!

Round and go round and never a need
For the spur or the whip. These galloping steeds
Neither hunger nor thirst nor hope. They go
For nothing to nowhere, like God and his rainbow.

Et dépêchez, chevaux de leur âme,
Déjà voici que la nuit qui tombe
Va réunir pigeon et colombe,
Loin de la foire et loin de madame.

Tournez, tournez! le ciel en velours
D'astres en or se vêt lentement.
Voici partir l'amante et l'amant.
Tournez au son joyeux des tambours.

Champ de foire de Saint-Gilles, août 1872

Go faster still, you horses of all souls.
The night is upon us, cold
Night that marries the pigeon to the dove
In one darkness, far from the fun.

Round and go round! Ever so slowly
The velvet of heaven is strewn with stars.
The lovers drift away. The horses keep going
In the bliss of abandonment, their song without words.

St. Giles fairground, August 1872

Malines

Vers les prés le vent cherche noise
Aux girouettes, détail fin
Du château de quelque échevin,
Rouge de brique et bleu d'ardoise,
Vers les prés clairs, les prés sans fin...

Comme les arbres des féeries,
Des frênes, vagues frondaisons,
Échelonnent mille horizons
À ce Sahara de prairies,
Trèfle, luzerne et blancs gazons.

Les wagons filent en silence
Parmi ces sites apaisés.
Dormez, les vaches! Reposez,
Doux taureaux de la plaine immense,
Sous vos cieux à peine irisés!

Le train glisse sans un murmure,
Chaque wagon est un salon
Où l'on cause bas et d'où l'on
Aime à loisir cette nature
Faite à souhait pour Fénelon.

Août 1872

Malines

Over the fields, the wind worries
Weathervanes, ornaments of a worthy's
Garish chateau—blood red
Brickwork, slate blue tiles—over
The endlessness, the shining fields…

Like trees in a fairy tale, ash trees
Undulate in billowing clouds of
Foliage, bright echelons, innumerable
Saharas of white landscape hovering
Above meadows of white clover.

In absolute silence the little train
Winds its way across Eden.
Cattle dream the dreams of cattle.
The sweet bullock of eternity
Grazes in midair.

The little train winds on.
Every car is a parlor car,
And the people speak in whispers,
Loving it, the Sunday school slow
Heaven here on earth.

                    August 1872

Birds in the Night

Birds in the Night

Vous n'avez pas eu toute patience,
Cela se comprend par malheur, de reste.
Vous êtes si jeune! Et l'insouciance,
C'est le lot amer de l'âge céleste!

Vous n'avez pas eu toute la douceur,
Cela par malheur d'ailleurs se comprend;
Vous êtes si jeune, ô ma froide sœur,
Que votre cœur doit être indifférent!

Aussi me voici plein de pardons chastes,
Non, certes! joyeux, mais très calme, en somme,
Bien que je déplore, en ces mois néfastes,
D'être, grâce à vous, le moins heureux homme.

You never had much in the way of patience.
That sums it up. As for the rest, well,
You're young, and the blithe insouciance
Of the young is, at the end of the day, cruel.

You were never exactly gentle either.
Understandable, I guess, but all the same,
Sad. So girlishly young, and yet so cold—
Frigid to the core, indifferent to the bone.

Just look at me: bursting with forgiveness,
Drunk with clemency...no, not drunk, but rather,
Stupefied. These past few infamous months,
Thanks to you, have made an imbecile of me.

Et vous voyez bien que j'avais raison
Quand je vous disais, dans mes moments noirs,
Que vos yeux, foyers de mes vieux espoirs,
Ne couvaient plus rien que la trahison.

Vous juriez alors que c'était mensonge
Et votre regard qui mentait lui-même
Flambait comme un feu mourant qu'on prolonge,
Et de votre voix vous disiez: « Je t'aime! »

Hélas! on se prend toujours au désir
Qu'on a d'être heureux malgré la saison…
Mais ce fut un jour plein d'amer plaisir,
Quand je m'aperçus que j'avais raison!

Surely you can see it now, just how right I was,
How right I was to have told you, in the black hours,
How your eyes, hearth of my first hope,
Glowed only with hatred, little twin cinders of hatred.

You swore up and down I was mistaken.
Meanwhile, the ash-heap of your face
Was set to burst into flame and finale:
"I love you," you'd say in that voice of yours, "I love you."

Christ! Can you see it now, how endless it is,
This desperate, blind seeking after happiness?
What a day that was, so bitter with pleasure,
Knowing for a certainty just how right I was!

Aussi bien pourquoi me mettrais-je à geindre?
Vous ne m'aimiez pas, l'affaire est conclue,
Et, ne voulant pas qu'on ose me plaindre,
Je souffrirai d'une âme résolue.

Oui! je souffrirai, car je vous aimais!
Mais je souffrirai comme un bon soldat
Blessé, qui s'en va dormir à jamais,
Plein d'amour pour quelque pays ingrat.

Vous qui fûtes ma Belle, ma Chérie,
Encor que de vous vienne ma souffrance,
N'êtes-vous donc pas toujours ma Patrie,
Aussi jeune, aussi folle que la France?

Well, that's that then, and no sense moaning.
You never *were* in love with me, I can see that now.
And don't expect me to go looking for pity.
My soul's my own. I'll suffer quietly.

And I *will* suffer. No worries there.
I'll suffer because I really did love you,
But with that kind of love a pathetic soldier
Feels as he dies forgotten in the mud.

And even though you left me dying in the mud,
You were ever my Beloved, my Dear One.
I can never not think of you as my native land,
My first home, Edenic and insane as France.

Or, je ne veux pas—le puis-je d'abord?
Plonger dans ceci mes regards mouillés.
Pourtant mon amour que vous croyez mort
A peut-être enfin les yeux dessillés.

Mon amour qui n'est que ressouvenance,
Quoique sous vos coups il saigne et qu'il pleure
Encore et qu'il doive, à ce que je pense,
Souffrir longtemps jusqu'à ce qu'il en meure,

Peut-être a raison de croire entrevoir
En vous un remords qui n'est pas banal,
Et d'entendre dire, en son désespoir,
À votre mémoire: ah! fi! que c'est mal!

No time for tears. I don't want them.
I want to see clearly, and I want you
To know my love is somewhat alive and sees you
Just as you are, just now, at this moment.

Love is the memory of itself loving,
And it bleeds. It weeps and reels
Under the blows and batterings. It goes
On, all the way to death, in real pain.

Could it have been something like, strange
As it seems, remorse I saw just now
Crossing your little face and your memory,
Crying aloud, "Oh hell, not again, not now!"

Je vous vois encor. J'entr'ouvris la porte.
Vous étiez au lit comme fatiguée.
Mais, ô corps léger que l'amour emporte,
Vous bondîtes nue, éplorée et gaie.

Ô quels baisers, quels enlacements fous!
J'en riais moi-même à travers mes pleurs.
Certes, ces instants seront, entre tous
Mes plus tristes, mais aussi mes meilleurs.

Je ne veux revoir de votre sourire
Et de vos bons yeux en cette occurrence
Et de vous, enfin, qu'il faudrait maudire,
Et du piège exquis, rien que l'apparence.

I can still see you. I pushed lightly
On the door, and there on the bed
Your little body slept inside itself,
Then came awake—naked, tearful, giddy.

Such kisses then, such a confusion of
White limbs in a tangle. I laughed and I cried.
No hour will ever again be so perfect,
No pleasure so perfectly sad.

I want nothing to do with you, now or ever.
I curse everything about you—your eyes,
Your smile, your exquisite cunning.
All I want is your body, that one morning.

Je vous vois encore! En robe d'été
Blanche et jaune avec des fleurs de rideaux.
Mais vous n'aviez plus l'humide gaîté
Du plus délirant de tous nos tantôts.

La petite épouse et la fille aînée
Était reparue avec la toilette
Et c'était déjà notre destinée
Qui me regardait sous votre voilette.

Soyez pardonnée! Et c'est pour cela
Que je garde, hélas! avec quelque orgueil,
En mon souvenir qui vous cajola
L'éclair de côté que coulait votre œil.

I can *still* see you! In your summer dress,
The yellow and white one, embroidered with bluebells,
But you weren't the same, not dewy and mischievous
As you'd been that morning, the wild one.

Little wifey, Papa's eldest child,
Had put her face back on again.
Simpering behind a breezy veil,
Our whole sad future frowned at me then.

God forgive you! And all because
Of a summer dress, I'll hold on
With a little pride to the memory
Of a shivering in the bluebells.

Par instants je suis le pauvre navire
Qui court démâté parmi la tempête,
Et, ne voyant pas Notre-Dame luire
Pour l'engouffrement en priant s'apprête.

Par instants je meurs la mort du pécheur
Qui se sait damné s'il n'est confessé,
Et, perdant l'espoir de nul confesseur,
Se tord dans l'Enfer qu'il a devancé.

Ô mais! par instants, j'ai l'extase rouge
Du premier chrétien, sous la dent rapace,
Qui rit à Jésus témoin, sans que bouge
Un poil de sa chair, un nerf de sa face!

Bruxelles–Londres.—Septembre–Octobre 1872

The light of Our Lady of Good Voyage
Finds not me. Time and again, I
Am the lost ship, the rudderless
Hulk awash in prayer.

Time and again I die, unconfessed,
The priestless sinner's irrevocable death.
In the knell of null and helpless,
I writhe in a prime hell.

Time and again too, I know
The martyr's bliss in the lion's mouth,
The calm of my King Jesus, the stillness
On the face of a good death.

Brussels–London.—September–October 1872

73

Aquarelles

Watercolors

Green

Voici des fruits, des fleurs, des feuilles et des branches,
Et puis voici mon cœur, qui ne bat que pour vous.
Ne le déchirez pas avec vos deux mains blanches
Et qu'à vos yeux si beaux l'humble présent soit doux.

J'arrive tout couvert encore de rosée
Que le vent du matin vient glacer à mon front.
Souffrez que ma fatigue, à vos pieds reposée,
Rêve des chers instants qui la délasseront.

Sur votre jeune sein laissez rouler ma tête
Toute sonore encore de vos derniers baisers;
Laissez-la s'apaiser de la bonne tempête,
Et que je dorme un peu puisque vous reposez.

Green

There's fruit and flowers, leaves and branches,
And then there's my heart—it belongs to you.
Don't tear it apart, it belongs to you.
Watch over it, keep it safe in your hands.

Here I stand, with the dew of the morning
Frozen to my face by the morning wind.
Lay me down at your little feet.
Lay me down into sweet memory.

Nuzzle me into your young breast
Like the last time, roll my head around.
Then let me rest a little. Let me
Sleep a little, as you are sleeping now.

Spleen

Les roses étaient toutes rouges,
Et les lierres étaient tout noirs.

Chère, pour peu que tu te bouges,
Renaissent tous mes désespoirs.

Le ciel était trop bleu, trop tendre,
La mer trop verte et l'air trop doux.

Je crains toujours,—ce qu'est d'attendre
Quelque fuite atroce de vous.

Du houx à la feuille vernie
Et du luisant buis je suis las,

Et de la campagne infinie
Et de tout, fors de vous, hélas!

Spleen

The roses were roses utterly,
The trellises black with ivy.

My love, the least glint of your hair
Wakes my despair.

The sky was too blue, too near,
The ocean soup-sweet as the air.

I'm frightened all the time. Very soon
Now, and cruelly, you'll be gone.

I'm tired of the English and their trees,
Tired of England, where "spleen" means only "spleen."

The waxy picturesque goes on forever.
But you, you were real. Nothing else matters.

Streets

I

    Dansons la gigue!

J'aimais surtout ses jolis yeux,
Plus clairs que l'étoile des cieux,
J'aimais ses yeux malicieux.

    Dansons la gigue!

Elle avait des façons vraiment
De désoler un pauvre amant,
Que c'en était vraiment charmant!

    Dansons la gigue!

Mais je trouve encore meilleur
Le baiser de sa bouche en fleur,
Depuis qu'elle est morte à mon cœur.

    Dansons la gigue!

Je me souviens, je me souviens
Des heures et des entretiens,
Et c'est le meilleur de mes biens.

    Dansons la gigue!

Soho

Streets

I

The jig! The jig!

Best of all I loved her eyes,
The glitter of malice in her eyes,
Cold starlight in a cloudless sky.

The jig! The jig!

She was ruin, she was a flawless
Desolation with plans, with a merciless
Charm about her wantonness.

The jig! The jig!

Dead to me now but still alive,
The flower of her mouth finds mine
And while we kiss, death is alive.

The jig! The jig!

I remember, I remember,
Hours folded into one hour,
And words like nothing said before.

The jig! The jig!

Soho

II

Ô la rivière dans la rue!
Fantastiquement apparue
Derrière un mur haut de cinq pieds,
Elle roule sans un murmure
Son onde opaque et pourtant pure,
Par les faubourgs pacifiés.

La chaussée est très large, en sorte
Que l'eau jaune comme une morte
Dévale ample et sans nuls espoirs
De rien refléter que la brume,
Même alors que l'aurore allume
Les cottages jaunes et noirs.

Paddington

II

Deep river in the little street!
Fantastic apparition
Behind a five-foot wall
Wordless undine
Undulant in suburban repose
Pure opacity.

Water yellow as death
The channel widens
Churning with no face
Other than fog
As day breaks
Blackening little houses.

Paddington

Child Wife

Vous n'avez rien compris à ma simplicité,
    Rien, ô ma pauvre enfant!
Et c'est avec un front éventé, dépité
    Que vous fuyez devant.

Vos yeux qui ne devaient refléter que douceur,
    Pauvre cher bleu miroir,
Ont pris un ton de fiel, ô lamentable sœur,
    Qui nous fait mal à voir.

Et vous gesticulez avec vos petits bras
    Comme un héros méchant,
En poussant d'aigres cris poitrinaires, hélas!
    Vous qui n'étiez que chant!

Car vous avez eu peur de l'orage et du cœur
    Qui grondait et sifflait,
Et vous bêlâtes vers votre mère—ô douleur!—
    Comme un triste agnelet.

Et vous n'avez pas su la lumière et l'honneur
    D'un amour brave et fort,
Joyeux dans le malheur, grave dans le bonheur,
    Jeune jusqu'à la mort!

Child Wife

You still don't get it. Oh, poor child,
     My simplicity
Is the animal you hunt in anger,
     Hopelessly.

Your eyes, which ought to be sugar-
     Blue Glimmerglass,
Look daggers at me. Oh, poor sister,
     It's sickening.

Your little shape's gone crazy.
     Poor spastic Camille,
Not long ago you were all arias.
     Now you shrill.

You were scared to death by something
     In the sky and in me.
Bleat, bleat, bleat, poor little lambkin.
     Run to mommy.

You still don't get it. There's an honor
     Beyond honor,
An innocence more lustrous than your innocence.
     You died old.

A Poor Young Shepherd

J'ai peur d'un baiser
Comme d'une abeille.
Je souffre et je veille
Sans me reposer.
J'ai peur d'un baiser!

Pourtant j'aime Kate
Et ses yeux jolis.
Elle est délicate,
Aux longs traits pâlis.
Oh! que j'aime Kate!

C'est Saint-Valentin!
Je dois et je n'ose
Lui dire au matin…
La terrible chose
Que Saint-Valentin!

Elle m'est promise,
Fort heureusement!
Mais quelle entreprise
Que d'être un amant
Près d'une promise!

J'ai peur d'un baiser
Comme d'une abeille.
Je souffre et je veille
Sans me reposer.
J'ai peur d'un baiser!

A Poor Young Shepherd

As frightened of fucking
As of bee stings,
I suffer and wait
Without sleeping,
Frightened of fucking!

All the same,
I love my Kate—
Her eyes, her delicate
Leggy whitenesses.
I love my Kate!

Valentine's Day!
I must and I dare not
Whisper in the morning
Terrible things.
Oh Valentine's Day!

She's promised to me,
And happily!
But it's dirty work
Being in love,
Being me.

As frightened of fucking
As of bee stings,
I suffer and wait
Without sleeping,
Frightened of fucking!

Beams

Elle voulut aller sur les flots de la mer,
Et comme un vent bénin soufflait une embellie,
Nous nous prêtâmes tous à sa belle folie,
Et nous voilà marchant par le chemin amer.

Le soleil luisait haut dans le ciel calme et lisse,
Et dans ses cheveux blonds c'étaient des rayons d'or,
Si bien que nous suivions son pas plus calme encor
Que le déroulement des vagues, ô délice!

Des oiseaux blancs volaient alentour mollement
Et des voiles au loin s'inclinaient toutes blanches.
Parfois de grands varechs filaient en longues branches,
Nos pieds glissaient d'un pur et large mouvement.

Elle se retourna, doucement inquiète
De ne nous croire pas pleinement rassurés;
Mais nous voyant joyeux d'être ses préférés,
Elle reprit sa route et portait haut sa tête.

Douvres–Ostende, à bord de la
Comtesse-de-Flandre, 4 avril 1873

Beams

She wanted to walk on water...
Soft breezes breathed a bright interval,
And we indulged her. There we were,
At the seamark, a mad patrol.

The sun stood tall in a clear sky.
In her hair, still another sun shone bright,
And we were in raptures, following her.
The waves uncoiled at her feet.

White birds circled overhead.
White sails tilted in the distance.
Black tresses of shining seaweed
Slavered our ankles. We were not afraid.

But worried we might be afraid,
She sweetly, only just slightly, turned around.
What she saw were joyful disciples.
And so she walked on, her head held high.

On board the *Countess of Flanders*,
Dover–Ostend, April 4, 1873

Translator's Afterword

Paul Verlaine, his genius taking refuge in the future, remains a hero.
—Mallarmé

Poetry is the afterlife of poems. Trailing wisps of glory and mishap, squalor and proprioception, they evanesce into the next utterance and the next, into circumstances not only beyond their control but, happily, beyond their first imagination. Thus in a swirling Parisian snow, on January 10, 1896, Mallarmé, delivering his funeral oration for Paul Verlaine, looked to the future of his late friend's poems and saw their genius safely sheltered in words yet to be written and in the company of writers yet to be born. Verlaine had always been ahead of his time. And by that I do not mean to characterize his genius as either prophetic or wildly innovative. He was a poet of the near—the nearest love, the nearest glass, the nearest glimmer of salvation. And his music is so simple, with rhymes and rhythms perfectly undisguised, that it seems to sound from some arcadian moment, long before the invention of writing or perhaps long after the final book has blown to ash. Verlaine was the forerunner of himself, a poet who had given his heart away in pursuit of his heart.

> De la musique avant toute chose...
>
> ("Art poétique")

Love sounds the music given, already and always just ahead. A poem is the first and following trace of the sound. And so it is that Verlaine seems purely a surrounding, sometimes called "Verlaine," disappearing and durable. In "Song of Myself," Walt Whitman opined, "If you want me again, look for me under your boot-soles." He meant to become grass, disappearing beneath the traveler's feet even as it stretches towards horizon. In "Tombeau de Paul Verlaine," written January 10, 1897, Mallarmé proposes the same for his departed master-friend:

> Verlaine? Il est caché parmi l'herbe, Verlaine...

What is the grass? It is a green thing hidden "parmi," among itself. The aftermath of Verlaine is Verlaine by other names, continuing. Resting inseparable from horizon, the poems speed and spread.

How shall we keep pace with Paul Verlaine? In poems, surely, careful always to be careless with desire, as was he, lest the nearest love become the last, and lest salvation settle into a threadbare paradise of ease. In "The Poet," Whitman's sage and reluctant advocate, Ralph Waldo Emerson, declared that "Language is fossil poetry." Keeping pace with Verlaine, we carry that declaration forward. Poetry is the afterlife of poems—a curio, a roadside chapel, an ossuary—unless another poem comes along, one as unsettled and unsettling as all the best before. The loving imperfections trust to luck, to a green horizon of haphazard.

> Et tout le reste est littérature...
>
>   ("Art poétique")

The unsure egoist is true to himself in glimmers and in flecks of time. True hedonism is tireless. Verlaine had no time for literature. He was too much in love with the poem at hand to trouble with judgment and meek adjustments. Even his darkness hurries beside his death, as profligate as daylight. The next poem cannot fail. One hundred years and more beyond Mallarmé's original elegy comes another *Tombeau de Paul Verlaine*, by Yves Bonnefoy, France's greatest living poet; and from it strides an exclamation, accomplice to Verlaine's escape:

> *Juges, au soir, les mots!*

In the evening, words are judges; but as to their justice, it's far too late to tell. And never mind. Daylight has escaped with the music of poems—"De la musique avant toute chose"—evanesced beyond control. Literature lags behind.

Where is Verlaine now? The question answers itself in its final word. And Verlaine was happy to say so, knowing that poems are made from poems that come after.

> *Maintenant, au gouffre de Bonheur!*

The "abyss of Happiness" images dimensionless refuge, its genius keeping time. Verlaine gave his heart away to happiness. The abyss will never fail him now.

Works Cited

Yves Bonnefoy. *Second Simplicity: New Poetry & Prose, 1991–2011* (trans. Hoyt Rogers). New Haven & London: Yale University Press, 2011.

Stéphane Mallarmé. *Divagations* (trans. Barbara Johnson). Cambridge, MA & London: The Belknap Press of Harvard University Press, 2007.

François Camoin

Donald Revell is Professor of English at the University of Nevada-Las Vegas. Winner of the PEN USA Translation Award for his translation of Rimbaud's *A Season in Hell* and two-time winner of the PEN USA Award for Poetry, he has also won the Academy of American Poets Lenore Marshall Prize and is a former fellow of the Ingram Merrill and Guggenheim Foundations. Additionally, he has twice been granted fellowships in poetry from the National Endowment for the Arts. Former editor-in-chief of *Denver Quarterly*, he now serves as poetry editor of *Colorado Review*. Revell lives in the desert south of Las Vegas with his wife, poet Claudia Keelan, and their children, Benjamin Brecht and Lucie Ming.

Songs without Words by Paul Verlaine
Translated by Donald Revell

Original cover artwork: *The Death of Pierrot* by Aubrey Beardsley,
from *The Savoy* (magazine), Volume 4, August 1898

Cover text set in Bernard Modern and Adobe Jensen Pro
Interior text set in Sanvito Pro and Adobe Jensen Pro

Cover and interior design by Ken Keegan

Omnidawn Publishing
Richmond, California
2013

Rusty Morrison & Ken Keegan, Senior Editors & Publishers
Cassandra Smith, Poetry Editor & Book Designer
Gillian Hamel, Poetry Editor & OmniVerse Managing Editor
Sara Mumolo, Poetry Editor
Peter Burghardt, Poetry Editor & Book Designer
Turner Canty, Poetry Editor
Liza Flum, Poetry Editor & Social Media
Sharon Osmond, Poetry Editor & Bookstore Outreach
Juliana Paslay, Fiction Editor & Bookstore Outreach Manager
Gail Aronson, Fiction Editor
RJ Ingram, Social Media
Pepper Luboff, Feature Writer
Craig Santos Perez, Media Consultant